A

FULL DESCRIPTION

OF THE

DAGUERREOTYPE

PROCESS;

AS PUBLISHED BY M. DAGUERRE.

ILLUSTRATED BY NUMEROUS WOOD CUTS.

EXTRACTED FROM THE AMERICAN REPERTORY, EDITED BY PROF. J. J. MAPES.

NEW-YORK:

FOR SALE BY J. R. CHILTON, 263 BROADWAY.

1840.

THE DAGUERREOTYPE.

We give below a description of this most interesting discovery, and take great pleasure in stating that several gentlemen of this city, among whom, we may name Dr. Chilton, President Morse, and Professor Draper, have fully succeeded in procuring fine specimens of photogenic drawing, by *means of this instrument.*   *Louis Jacques. Mandé*

Translated from the original paper of L. J. M. Daguerre, (the inventor,) by J. S. MEMES, L L. D.

Practical Description of the Daguerréotype.   Material to be employed in the photogenic process.   Five steps of the process explained.   Polishing the white coating with Iodine.   The Camera.   Mercurial process. Fixing the impression, with descriptions of the Apparatus.

THE designs are executed upon thin plates of silver, plated on copper.   Although the copper serves principally to support the silver foil, the combination of the two metals tends to the perfection of the effect. The silver must be the purest that can be procured.   As to the copper, its thickness ought to be sufficient to maintain the perfect smoothness and flatness of the plate, so that the images may not be distorted by the warping of the tablet; but unnecessary thickness beyond this is to be avoided on account of the weight.   The thickness of the two metals united, ought not to exceed that of a stout card.

The process is divided into five operations :

1. The first consists in polishing and cleaning the plate, in order to prepare it for receiving the sensitive coating, upon which the light traces the design.

2. The second is to apply this coating.

3. The third is the placing the prepared plate properly in the camera obscura to the action of light, for the purpose of receiving the image of nature.

4. The fourth brings out this image, which at first is not visible on the plate being withdrawn from the camera obscura.

5. The fifth and last operation has for its object to remove the sensitive coating on which the design is first impressed, because this coating would continue to be affected by the rays of light, a property which would necessarily and quickly destroy the picture.

FIRST OPERATION.
Preparing the Plate.

The requisites for this operation are of :

A small phial containing olive oil.

Some very finely carded cotton.

A small quantity of very fine pumice powder, ground with the utmost care, tied up in a bag of muslin, sufficiently thin to allow the powder to pass through when the bag is shaken.

A phial of nitric acid, diluted with water in the proportion of one pint of acid to sixteen pints of distilled water. These proportions express volume, not weight.

A frame of iron wire upon which to place the plate, in order that it may be heated by means of a spirit lamp.

Lastly, a small spirit lamp.

As already stated, these photographic delineations are executed upon siver plated on copper. The size of the plate will depend of course on the dimensions of the camera. We must begin by polishing it carefully. To accomplish this, the surface of the silver is powdered all over with the pumice, by shaking the bag without touching the plate.

Next, with some cotton dipped in a little olive oil, the operator rubs the plate gently, rounding his strokes, as represented, Fig. 2. beginning from C. During this operation the plate must be laid flat upon several folds of paper, care being taken to renew these from time to time, that the tablet be not twisted from any inequality in the support.

The pumice must be renewed and the cotton changed several times. The mortar employed for preparing the pumice must be of porphyry. The powder is afterwards finished by grinding upon polished glass, with a glass muller, and very pure water. And lastly, it must be perfectly dried. It will be readily apprehended of what importance it is to attend to these directions, since upon the high polish of the silver depends in a great measure the beauty of the future design. When the plate is well polished, it must next be cleaned by powdering it all over once more with pumice, and rubbing with dry cotton, always rounding and crossing the strokes, for it is impossible to obtain a true surface by any other motion of the hand. A little pledget of cotton is now rolled up and moistened with the diluted acid already mentioned, by applying the cotton to the mouth of the phial and inverting it, pressing gently, so that the centre only of the cotton may be wetted, and but slightly, care being taken not to allow any acid to touch the fingers. The surface of the plate is now rubbed *equally* all over with the acid applied by the pledget of cotton. Change the cotton and keep rubbing, rounding as before, that the acid may be equally spread, yet in so small a quantity as just to skim the surface, so to speak. If, as frequently happens, the acid run into small drops from the high polish, change the cotton repeatedly and break down the globules as quickly as possible, but always by gently rubbing, for if allowed to rest or run upon the plate they will leave stains. It will be seen when the acid has been properly diffused, from the appearance of a thin veil spread regularly over the whole surface of the plate. Once more powder over pumice, and clean it with fresh cotton, rubbing as before, but very slightly.

The plate is now to be subjected to a strong heat. It is placed upon the wire frame, (Fig. 1, both views,) the silver upwards. The spirit lamp is applied below the hand, moving it round, the flame touching and playing upon the copper. This operation being continued at least five minutes, a white strong coating is formed all over the surface of the silver, if the lamp has been made to traverse with proper regularity; the lamp is now withdrawn. A fire of charcoal may be used instead of the lamp, and is perhaps preferable, the operation being sooner completed. In this latter case the wire frame is unnecessary, because the plate may be held by one corner with pincers, and so held over the fire, moving it at the same time till all is equally heated, and the veil appear as before described. The plate is now to be cooled *suddenly* by placing it on a cold substance, such as a mass of metal or stone, or best of all a marble table. When perfectly cold, it is to be again polished, an operation speedily performed, since the gummy appearance merely has to be removed, which is done by the dry pumice and cotton repeated several times, changing the cotton frequently. The polishing being thus completed, the operation of the acid is to be repeated three different times, dry pumice being powdered over the plate each time, and polished off very gently with the cotton, which must be very clean, care being taken not to breathe upon the plate or to touch it with the fingers, or even with the cotton upon which the fingers have rested, for the slightest stain upon the surface will cause a defect in the drawing.

When the plate is not intended for immediate use, the last operation of the acid is not performed. This allows any number of plates to be kept prepared up to the last slight operation, and they may be purchased in this state if required. It is, however, indispensable that a last operation by acid as described, be performed on every plate, immediately before it be placed in the camera. Lastly, every particle of dust is removed by gently cleaning the whole edges and back also with cotton.

SECOND OPERATION.
Coating the plate.

For this operation, we require :
The box represented, Figs. 7 and 8.
The small board, Fig. 3.
Four small metallic bands, the same substance as the plates.
A small handle, Fig. 5. and a box of small tacks.
A phial of iodine.
The plate is first to be fixed upon the board by means of the metallic bands with their small catches and tacks, as represent Fig. 3. The iodine is now put into the little dish, D, at the bottom of the box, Figs. 7 and 8. It is necessary to divide the iodine into pieces, in order to render the exhalation the more extensively and more equally diffused, otherwise it would form circles in the centre of the plate, which would destroy this essential requisite. The board is now fitted into its position, the plate face downwards, the whole being supported by small brackets projecting from the four corners of the box, the lid of which, G, is then closed. In this position the apparatus remains till the vaporization of the iodine, which is condensed upon the plate, has covered its surface with a fine coating of a yellow gold color. If this operation be protracted, the gold color passes into violet, which must be avoided, because in this state the coating is not so sensitive to the impressions of light. On the contrary, if the coating be too pale, the image of nature in the camera will be too faint to produce a good picture. A decided gold color—nothing more—nothing less—is the only assurance that the ground of the future picture is duly prepared

The time for this cannot be determined, because it depends upon several circumstances. Of these two the principal are the temperature of the apartment, and the state of the apparatus. The operation should be left entirely to spontaneous evaporation of the iodine—or at all events no other heat should be used than what can be applied through the temperature of the room in which the operation takes place. It is also very important that the temperature of the inside of the box be equal to that of the air outside, for otherwise, a deposition of moisture takes place upon the plate, a circumstance most injurious to the final result. Secondly, as respects the state of the apparatus; the oftener it has been used, the less time is required, because in this case, the interior of the box being denetrated with the vapors of iodine, these arise from all sides, conpensing thus more equally and more rapidly upon the surface of the plate, a very important advantage. Hence it is of consequence to leave always a small quantity of iodine in the cup, and to protect this latter from damp. Hence, likewise, it is obvious that an apparatus of this kind which has been some time in use, is preferable to a new box, for in the former the operation is always more expeditiously performed.

Since from these causes the time cannot be fixed, *a priori*, and may vary from five minutes to half an hour, rarely more, unless the weather be too cold, means must be adopted for examining the plate from time to time. In these examinations it is important not to allow the light to fall directly upon the plate. Also, if it appear that the color is deeper on one side of the plate than the other, to equalize the coating the board must be replaced, not exactly in its former position, but turned one quarter round at each inspection. In order to accomplish these repeated examinations without injuring the sensibility of the ground or coating, the process must be conducted in a darkened apartment into which the light is admitted sideways, never from the roof—the door left a little ajar answers best. When the operator would inspect the plate, he raises the lid of the box, and lifting the board with both hands turns up the plate quickly, and very little light suffices to shew him the true color of the coating. If too pale, the plate must be instantly replaced, till it attain the proper gold tone; but if this tint be passed, the coating is useless, and the operations must be repeated from the commencement of the first.

From description this operation may perhaps seem difficult, but with a little practice one comes to know pretty nearly the precise interval necessary to produce the true tone of color, and also to inspect the plate with great rapidity, so as not to allow time for the light to act.

When the coating has reached the proper tone of yellow, the plate to which it is fitted, is slipped into the frame, (Fig.13.) and thus adjusted at once in the camera. In this transference care must be taken to protect the plate from the light; a taper should be used, and even with this precaution, the operation ought to be performed as quickly as possible, for a taper will leave traces of its action if continued for any length of time.

We pass now to the third operation, that of the camera. If possible the one should *immediately* succeed the other, the longest interval between the second and third ought not to exceed an hour. Beyond this space the action of the iodine and silver no longer possesses the requisite photogenic properties.

Observanda.—Before making use of the box, the operator should clean it thoroughly, turning it bottom upwards, in order to empty it of all the particles of iodine which may have escaped from the cup, avoiding at the same time touching the iodine with the fingers. During the operation of coating, the cup ought to be covered with a piece of gauze stretched on a ring. The gause regulates the evaporation of the iodine, and also prevents the compression of the air on the lid being shut from scattering the particles of iodine, some of which reaching the plate, would leave the large stains on the coating. For the same reason the top should always be let down with the greatest gentleness, not to raise the dust in the inside, the particles of which being charged with the vapor of the iodine, would certainly reach and damage the plate.

THIRD OPERATION.
The Camera.

The apparatus required in this operation is limited to the camera obscura. (Figs. 14 and 15.)

This third operation is that in which by means of light, acting through the camera, nature impresses an image of herself on the photographic plate, enlightened by the sun, for then the operation is more speedy. It is easy to conceive that this operation, being accomplished only through the agency of light, will be the more rapid in proportion as the objects, whose photographic images are to be delineated, stand exposed to a strong illumination, or in their own nature present bright lines and surfaces.

After having placed the camera in front of the landscape, or facing any other object of which it may be desirable to obtain a representation, the first essential is a perfect adjustment of the focus, that is to say, making your arrangements so as to obtain the outlines of the subject with great neatness. This is accomplished by advancing or withdrawing the frame of the obscured glass which receives the images of natural objects. The adjustment being made with satisfactory precision, the moveable part of the camera is fixed by the proper means, and the obscured glass being withdrawn, its place is supplied by the apparatus, with the plate attached as already described, and the whole secured by small brass screws. The light is of course all this time excluded by the inner doors; these are now opened by means of two semi-circles (see illustration) and the plate is disposed ready to receive its proper impressions. It remains only to open the aperture of the camera, and to consult a watch.

This latter is a task of some nicety, as nothing is visible, and as it is quite impossible to determine the time necessary for producing a design, this depending entirely on the intensity of the light on the objects, the imagery of which is to be reproduced. At Paris, for example, this varies from three to thirty minutes.

It is likewise to be remarked, that the seasons as well as the hour of the day, exert considerable influence on the celerity of the operation. The most favorable time is from seven to three o'clock; and a drawing which, in the months of June and July at Paris, may be taken in three or four minutes, will require five or six in May or August, seven or eight in April and September, and so on in proportion to the progress of the season. These are only general data for very bright or strongly illuminated objects, for it often happens that twenty minutes are necessary in the most favorable months, when the objects are entirely in shadow.

After what has just been said, it will readily occur to the reader that it is impossible to specify with precision the exact length of time necessary to obtain photographic designs; practice is the only sure guide and with this advantage, one soon comes to appreciate the required time very correctly. The latitude is of course a fixed element in this calculation. In the south of France, for example, and generally in all those countries in which light has great intensity, as Spain, Italy, &c: we can easily understand that these designs must be obtained with greater promptitude than in more northern regions. It is, however, very important not to exceed the time necessary, in different circumstances, for producing a design, because, in that case, the lights in the drawing will not be clear, but will be blackened by a too prolonged solarization. If, on the contrary, the time has been too short, the sketch will be very vague, and without the proper details.

Supposing that he has failed in a first trial, by withdrawing the tablet too soon, or by leaving it too long exposed, the operator, in either case, should commence with another plate immediately; the second trial, being corrected by the first, almost insures success. It is even useful, in order to acquire experience, to make some essays of this kind.

In this stage of the process, it is the same as for the coating; we must hasten to the next operation. When the plate is withdrawn from the camera, it should immediately be subjected to the subsequent process; there ought not, to be at most a longer interval than an hour between the third and fourth operations; but one is always surest of disengaging the images when no space has been allowed to intervene.

FOURTH OPERATION.
Mercurial or disengaging process.

Here are required:

A phial of mercury, containing at least 3 oz.

A lamp with spirit of wine.

The apparatus represented by Figs. 16, 17, and 18.

A glass funnel with a long neck.

By means of the funnel the mercury is poured into the cup C at the bottom of the larger vessel. The quantity must be sufficient to cover the bulb of a thermometer F. Afterwards, and throughout the remaining operations, no light save a taper can be used.

The board with the plate affixed is now to be withdrawn from the frame already described as adapted to the camera, and figured Fig. 13. The board and plate are placed within the ledges of the black iron vessel Fig. 16, at an angle of 45° the tablet with sketch downwards, so that it can be seen through the glass G. The top A is then gently put down, so as not to raise up particles of the mercury.

16

When all things are thus disposed, the spirit lamp is lighted, and placed under the cup containing mercury. The operation of the lamp is allowed to continue till the thermometer, the bulb of which is covered by the mercury, indicates a temperature of 60° centigrade. The lamp is then immediately withdrawn; if the thermometer has risen rapidly, it will continue to rise without the aid of a lamp, but this elevation ought not to exceed 75° centigrade.

The impress of the image of nature exists upon the plate, but it is invisible. It is not till after the lapse of several minutes that the faint tracery of objects begins to appear, of which the operator assures himself by looking through the glass G, by the light of a taper, using it cautiously that its rays may not fall upon, and injure the nascent images of the sketch. The operation is continued till the thermometer sink to 45° centigrade; the plate is then withdrawn, and this operation completed.

When the objects have been strongly illuminated, or when the action in the camera has been continued rather too long, it happens that this fourth operation is completed before the thermometer has fallen even to 55° centigrade. One may always know this, however, by observing the sketch through the glass

It is necessary after each operation to clean the inside of the · apparatus carefully, to remove the slight coating of mercury adhering to it. When the apparatus has to be packed for the purpose of removal, the mercury is withdrawn by the small cock E, inclining the vessel to that side.

One may now examine the sketch by a feeble light in order to be certain that the processes hitherto have succeeded. The plate is now detached from the board, and the little bands of metal which held it there are carefully cleaned with pumice and water after each experiment, a precaution rendered necessary from the coating both of iodine and of mercury which they have acquired. The plate is now deposited in the grooved box (Fig. 9.) until it undergoes the fifth and last operation. This may be deferred if not convenient; for the sketch may now be kept for months in its present state without alteration, provided it be not too frequently inspected by the full daylight.

FIFTH OPERATION.

Fixing the impression.

The object of this final process is to remove from the tablet the coating of iodine, which, continuing to decompose by light would otherwise speedily destroy the design when too long exposed. For this operation the requisites are :

A saturated solution of common salt, or a weak solution of hyposulphite of pure soda.

The apparatus represented Fig. 19, first and second views.

Two square troughs, sheet copper, Fig. 21, both views.

A vessel for distilled water, Fig. 23.

In order to remove the coating of iodine, common salt is put into a bottle with a wide mouth, which is filled one-fourth with salt, and three-fourths with pure water. To dissolve the salt, shake the bottle, and when the whole forms a saturated solution, filter through paper. This solution is prepared in large quantities beforehand, and kept in corked bottles.

Into one of the square troughs, pour the solution, filling it to the height of an inch; into the other pour in like manner the water. The solution of salt may be replaced by one of hyposulphite of soda, which is even preferable, because it removes the iodine entirely, which the saline solution does not always accomplish, especially, when the sketches have been laid aside for some time between the fourth and fifth operations. It does not require to be warmed, and a less quantity is required.

First, the plate is placed in common water, poured into a trough, plunging and withdrawing it immediately—the surface merely requiring to be moistened—then plunge it into the saline solution, which latter would act upon the drawing if not previously hardened by the washing in pure water. To assist the effect of the saline solutions, the plate is moved about in them by means of a little hoop of copper wire, Fig. 22. When the yellow color has quite disappeared, the plate is lifted up with both hands, care being taken not to touch the drawing, and plunged again into the first trough of pure water.

Next, the apparatus, Fig.19, (two views) and the bottle Fig. 23, having been previously prepared, made very clean, and the bottle filled with distilled water, the plate is withdrawn from the trough, and being instantly placed upon the inclined plane, Fig. 19, distilled water, hot, but not boiling, is made to flow in a stream over its whole surface, carrying away every remaining portion of the saline wash.*

Not less than a quart of distilled water is required when the design is of the dimensions indicated in the engraving, $8\frac{1}{2}$ by $6\frac{1}{2}$ inches. The drops of water remaining on the plate must be removed by forcibly blowing upon it, for otherwise in drying they would leave stains on the drawing. Hence also will appear the necessity of using very pure water, for if, in this last washing, the liquid contain an admixture of foreign substances, they will be deposited on the plate, leaving behind numerous and permanent stains. To be assured of the purity of the water, let a drop fall upon a piece of polished metal; evaporate by heat, and if no stain be left the water is pure. Distilled water is always sufficiently pure without this trial.

After this washing the drawing is finished; it remains only to preserve it from the dust and from the vapors that might tarnish the silver. The mercury by the action of which the images are rendered visible, is partially decomposed; it resists washing, by adhesion to the silver, but cannot endure the slightest rubbing.

To preserve the sketches then, place them in squares of strong pasteboard, with a glass over them, and frame the whole in wood. They are thenceforth unalterable even by the sun's light.

In traveling, the collector may preserve his sketches in a box similar to the one Fig. 9, and for greater security may close the joints of the lid† with a collar of paper. It is necessary to state that the same

---

* If hyposulphite has been used, the distilled water need not be as so hot as when common salt has been employed.

†The author made attempts to preserve his sketches by means of different varnishes obtained from succinum, copal, india rubber, wax, and various resins; but

plate may be employed for several successive trials, provided the silver be not polished through to the copper. But it is very important after each trial to remove the mercury immediately, by using the pumice powder with oil, and changing the cotton frequently during the operation. If this be neglected, the mercury finally adheres to the silver, and fine drawings cannot be obtained if this amalgam be present. They always in this case want firmness, neatness, and vigor of outline and general effect.

EXPLANATION OF THE APPARATUS USED IN THE PROCESS.

The translator would add from his own experience, that two requisites are indispensable in these experiments: exquisite polish of the plate, and extreme cleanliness in all the operations; dust and stains on the tablet make large blanks in the drawing.

SCALE.

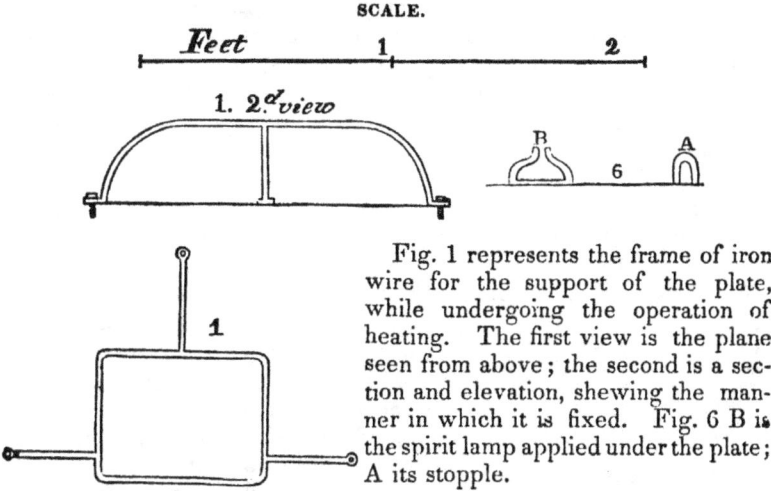

Fig. 1 represents the frame of iron wire for the support of the plate, while undergoing the operation of heating. The first view is the plane seen from above; the second is a section and elevation, shewing the manner in which it is fixed. Fig. 6 B is the spirit lamp applied under the plate; A its stopple.

Fig. 2. The plate of plated silver on which the photographic design is made. The dimensions according to the scale are eight and a quarter inches by six inches four tenths. To operate upon plates of larger dimensions requires all the apparatus to be enlarged, for the same camera which admits light sufficient for such a plate has its intensity too much diminished, when a greater focal distance with the

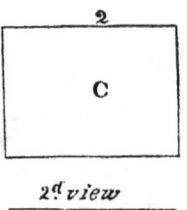

he has observed, that by the application of any varnish whatsoever, the lights in these sketches were considerably weakened, and at the same time the deeper tones were hidden. To this disadvantage, was added the still greater injury from the decomposition of the mercury by all the varnishes tried; this effect, which did not become apparent till after the lapse of two or three months, terminated in a total destruction of the forms of the objects represented. Even had this not been the case, the author would have deemed it a sufficient reason for rejecting all varnishes, that they injured the vigor and clearness of the lights. The quality most to be desired in the new art is this intensity of tone in the contrast of the lights and shadows.

same aperture, and consequently same number of rays, spread over a larger surface. In polishing the plate, begin at C, and strike circularly outwards to the circumference. Vary the direction, however, and invert the process. Always press lightly and evenly. Fig. 2, second view, is the plate seen edgeways: the lines represent (nearly) its thickness. Fig 4, muslin bag, with pumice powder.

Fig. 3. The little board or wooden tablet upon which the plate is fixed for the succeeding operations after the first one of polishing. It

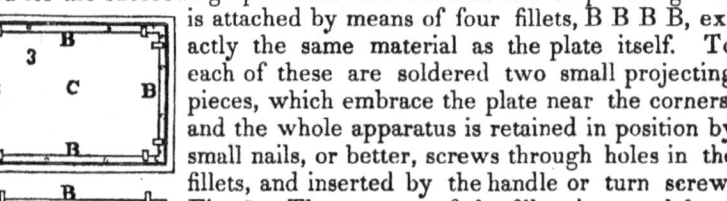

is attached by means of four fillets, B B B B, exactly the same material as the plate itself. To each of these are soldered two small projecting pieces, which embrace the plate near the corners, and the whole apparatus is retained in position by small nails, or better, screws through holes in the fillets, and inserted by the handle or turn screw, Fig. 5. The purpose of the fillets is not solely to fix the plate, their more important use is to serve as a kind of frame to it, while undergoing the second process; the application of the iodine : without these, the cooling of iodine would not be equally diffused, for the vapor would condense more rapidly along the edges, and consequently, the coating would be too thin in the centre and too thick round the circumference. It is perhaps not easy to explain so as to satisfy all; but the experimental part is not the less certain. Fig. 3, second view, thickness of the board.

Fig. 7. Section of the box for iodine, used in the second operation.

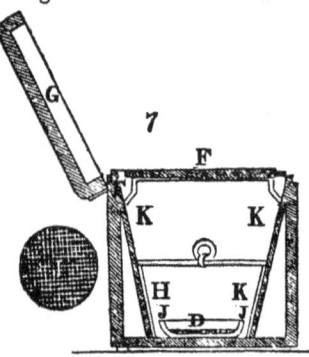

The section is supposed to pass down the middle of the apparatus by the line A B, Fig. 8, which represents the same seen from above. C is a small lid, which fits accurately the interior, dividing the whole into two chambers. It is used at all times, except when the operator is actually employed in coating the tablet. Its use is to concentrate the vapor of the iodine, and preserve the whole in a state for equally and rapidly diffusing the vapor, when the plate has been introduced.

D is the capsule or little cup in which the iodine is placed. E the small board with the plate attached, face downwards. Four small projecting supports, F, receive the four angles and retain the plate in the most favorable position for receiving the vaporization of the iodine as it rises upwards. Of course the cover C is withdrawn. G is the

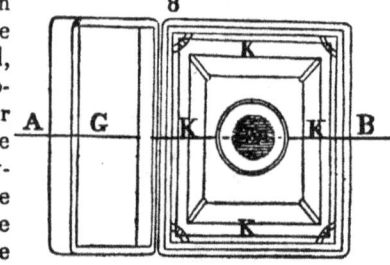

box lid, always shut, except when the plate is to be withdrawn for examination. H supports for C. K, tapering sides all round, forming a funnel-shaped box within the other; the funnel-shaped interior diffuses the vapors of iodine, which thus spread as they rise. J, circle of gauze, stretched over a ring, and placed upon the cup with the iodine. The vapor of which rising through this light covering flows up equally, and not in clouds, also the gauze prevents the particles of this substance from flying about and probably injuring the plate.

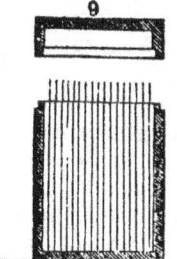

Fig. 9. Case for preserving the plates from injury, either before or after they have been impressed with images. They slip into grooves formed into two opposite sides of the case, and at some little distance apart, so that the plates cannot touch in any part of their surfaces. If filled with plates, that have designs, the case should be wrapped in paper, or better, cloth, to preserve them from dust and light. In traveling, this precaution is always necessary.

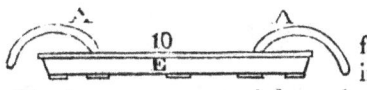

Figs. 10, 11, 12, and 13, represent four different positions of the frame into which the plate with its wooden tablet is put, on removal from the iodine process. The object of the apparatus is twofold:—to adapt the plate to the camera obscura, and to protect the iodine coating from the action of light to the moment in which it receives the focal image.

A, Half circles which open and shut the doors, B B.

C, Fig. 13. The plate with its wooden tablet fitted into the frame:

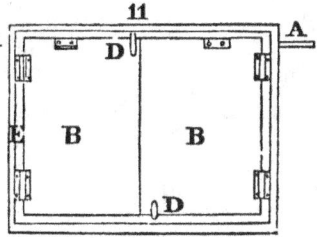

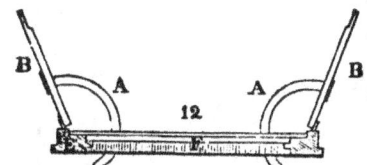

back view of the *plate* fronting inwards, the door shut upon it.

D, screws to fix the tablet and plate and to stop the doors.

E, thickness of the frame.

F, Fig. 12. Plate: the whole represents the arrangement for receiving the photogenic impressions on the plate, the doors being open, the focal image falls upon the prepared plate, and leaves its impress penciled there by the rays of light proceeding from the natural objects.

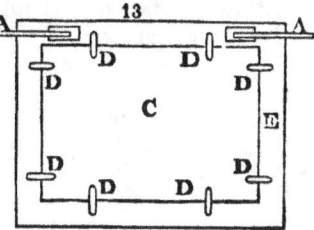

The camera obscura, as adapted to photogenic delineation is shown Fig. 14, which is a perpendicular section lengthways.

A, a ground glass by which the focus is adjusted. It is then removed, and the photographic plate substituted, as in C, Fig. 15. B, a mirror for observing the effect of objects, and selecting points of view. For these purposes it is inclined at an angle of 45°, by means of the support L. To adjust the focus, the mirror is put down altogether, and the ground glass A used. The

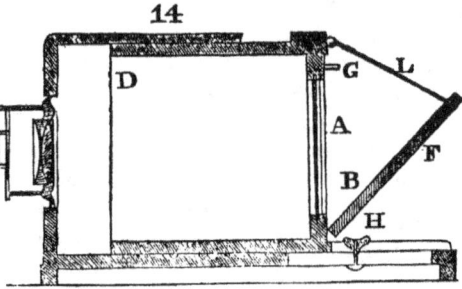

focus is easily adjusted by means of the sliding frame, as represented in the plate, placing the screws on the double box D, and the projection E : when the focus is adjusted, it is fixed in position by the screw H. The mirror is retained in its place by hooks at F, which catch the eyes at G.

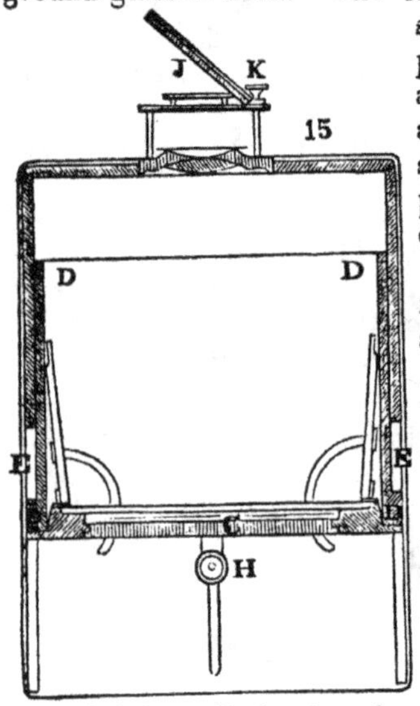

The object glass is achromatic and periscopic. Its diameter is 21 millimetres, and its focal distance 38 centimetres. In Eng. measure, $\dfrac{21 \times 38}{1900}$ in. and $\dfrac{38 \times 39}{100}$ in. which can easily be reduced.

This instrument has the disadvantage of reversing the objects. This can indeed be easily obviated by substituting another mirror outside, as K J, Fig 15. This arrangement, however, injures the effect on the photographic plate from the loss of light. It is therefore not to be employed unless when the operator has time to spare. It increases the time of the operation by one-third of the whole.

Figs. 16, 17, and 18 represent three views of the same apparatus—that used for the fourth operation—submitting the plate to the vapor of mercury.

Fig. 16. Section of the apparatus.

Fig. 17. Front view of the same.

Fig. 18. Right side in which the thermometer is placed.

A, Lid of the apparatus.

B, Blackboard with grooves to receive the small board and plate.

C, Cup containing mercury.

D, Lamp with spirit of wine.

E, Small cock inserted at an angle, through which the mercury is withdrawn after the operation.

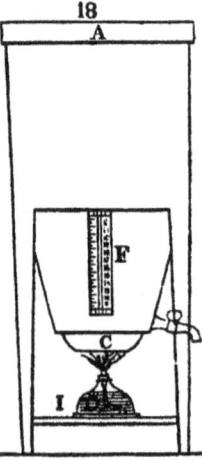

F, Thermometer.

G, Glass through which to inspect the operation.

H, Tablet with the plate as removed from the camera.

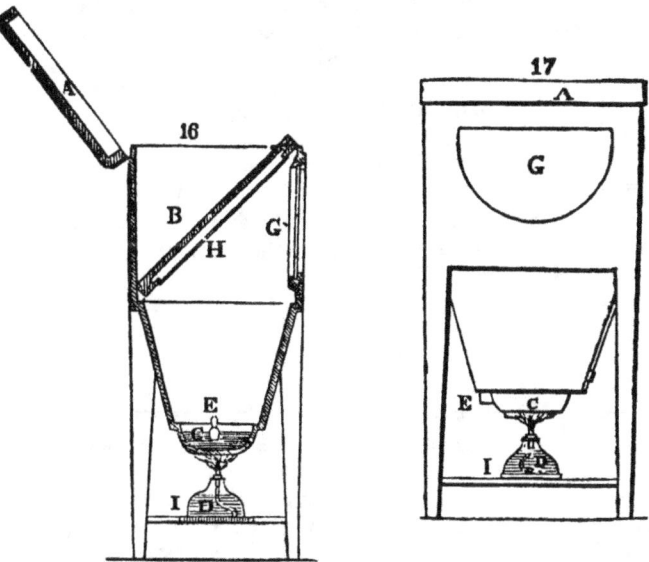

I, Stand for the spirit lamp which is placed within the ring N, so as be under the centre of the cup.

All the interior of this apparatus should be black and varnished.

Figs. 19, 20, 21, 22 and 23, represent various apparatus for the last operation of washing the plate.

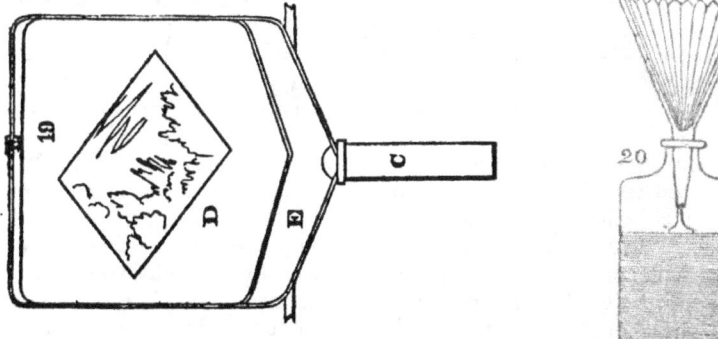

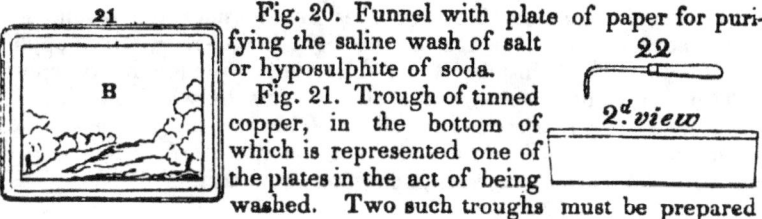

Fig. 20. Funnel with plate of paper for purifying the saline wash of salt or hyposulphite of soda.

Fig. 21. Trough of tinned copper, in the bottom of which is represented one of the plates in the act of being washed. Two such troughs must be prepared

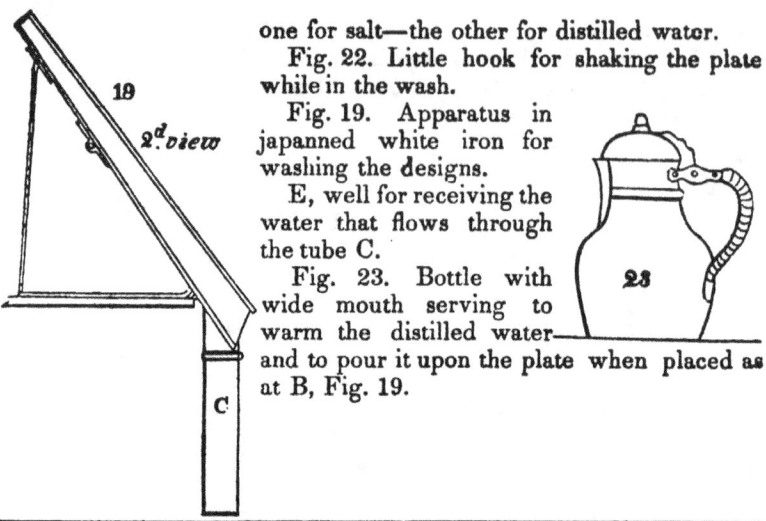

one for salt—the other for distilled water.

Fig. 22. Little hook for shaking the plate while in the wash.

Fig. 19. Apparatus in japanned white iron for washing the designs.

E, well for receiving the water that flows through the tube C.

Fig. 23. Bottle with wide mouth serving to warm the distilled water and to pour it upon the plate when placed as at B, Fig. 19.

IMPROVEMENTS IN THE DAGUERREOTYPE.—At the late meetings of the Academy of Sciences, much attention has been given to the various improvements made in the Daguerreotype, which instrument seems to have attracted the very active notice of scientific men in general. In the first place, the Baron Seguier exhibited an instrument of this kind constructed by himself, but with ingenious modifications, having for their objects, diminution in size and weight, and the simplification in other respects of the entire apparatus. M. Seguier expressed himself satisfied that several of the conditions, which have been announced as required for the success of the process, may be dispensed with; and stated his intention of devoting himself to a still further simplification of the apparatus, so as, at least, to make it more portable, more easy of use, and less expensive. His improvements have likewise been directed to rendering the operations of photography practicable in the open country, even those delicate ones, which seem at present to require protection against too strong a light. M. Arago afterwards laid before the academicians an objective glass, constructed by M. Cauche, with the view of *redressing* the image obtained in the Daguerreotype, which is now presented *reversed*, a circumstance that, in many cases, destroys the resemblance of places and monuments. The Abbé Moignat gave an account of experiments made by himself, in conjunction with M. Soleil, for the purpose of introducing the light of oxyhydrogen gas, as the principle of illumination to the objects intended to be represented by the instrument. As yet, these experiments have been unsuccessful; but M. Arago does not consider the results hitherto obtained as decisive against the light in question, when applied to the plate itself, instead of the objects to be rendered. A report has also been made on the results of a process, by which M. Bayard is enabled to take impressions on paper. This discovery is described as important; but, as the process is kept secret, we are unable to say how far it differs from, or is an improvement on, that of Mr. Fox Talbot.   **17**

OBSERVATIONS.

The preceding pages describe fully the process of M. Daguerre—a strict adherence to which will enable almost any
person to produce beautiful specimens; and it affords us great
pleasure to state that, since the knowledge of this wonderful
discovery reached this country, some of our scientific men have
been engaged in repeating the experiments, and have produced
some good results.

It could not, however, be supposed that the peculiar spirit of
American enterprise would rest satisfied with this; and, accord-
ingly, no sooner had those engaged in the experiments fully satisfied themselves that the process was practically given, than
they almost immediately conceived it possible to effect similar
results by more simple and less expensive means; and we are
happy to state that the results of their experiments have estab-
lished the following facts, viz :—

1. That instead of the costly combination of glasses, recommended by M. Daguerre, a single Meniscus glass has produced
as exact and brilliant results as we have yet seen, and requires
less time.

2. From a number of experiments it has been proved, that
the use of dilute nitric acid can be dispensed with, as several
fine proofs have been produced without its use. This renders
the process much more simple; for the application of the acid
has heretofore been considered one of the nicest points in the
preparation of the plate, as, if it be unequally applied, it prevents the plate from acquiring the uniform golden color when
exposed in the iodine box. In dispensing with the use of nitric
acid, all that is required is to finish the polish of the plate,
with dry, well levigated, and washed rotten stone; after which,
the plate should be carefully rubbed off with dry cotton.

3. The iodine box, recommended by M. Daguerre, is entirely
too deep, for it requires from 15 to 30 minutes exposure of the
plate before the proper color is produced. The box should be
about four inches deep, with a tray, an inch deep, that will fit
into the bottom of it. Upon this tray the iodine is to be spread,
and then covered with a double thickness of fine gauze, or vel-

vet, which is to be tacked to the upper edge of the tray ; supports are then to be fastened in each corner of the box, at such a height as that the plate can be lowered to within an inch of the gauze. A box constructed on this plan will produce the proper golden color, on the plate, in one or two minutes. This modification of the iodine box was suggested by Mr. Seager, who has used it satisfactorily for some time past.

4. The ingenuity displayed by some of our mechanics in the manufacture of the plates, gives us every reason to believe that, ere long, they will be furnished with almost the requisite polish, at a reasonable price. Should they succeed in doing this, it will save the experimenter several hours of manual labor, in the preparation of the plate, as nothing then will be required but the finishing polish, with prepared rotten stone, mentioned above.

TABLE OF GENERAL RULES
FOR EXPOSURE OF THE PLATE IN THE CAMERA, IN TAKING EXTERIOR VIEWS.

☞ The following Table is compiled partly from observation, and partly from analogy, and applies only to the period from the month of October to February. The observations were made upon ordinary city views.

STATE OF THE WEATHER.	HOURS OF THE DAY.						
	8	9	10	11 to 1	1 to 2	2 to 3	3 and after
Very brilliant and clear, wind steady from W. or N. W., very deep blue sky, and absence of red rays at sunrise or sunset. Time employed......................	15 MINUTES.	8 MINUTES.	6 MINUTES.	5 MINUTES.	6 MINUTES.	7 MINUTES.	12 to 30 MINUTES.
Clear, wind from S. W., moderately cold, but a slight perceptible vapor in comparison with above. Time employed...............	16	12	7	6	7	8	15 to 40
Sunshine, but rather hazy, shadows not hard, nor clearly defined. Time employed	25	18	14	12	14	16	25 to 40
Sun always obscured by light clouds, but lower atmosphere, clear from haze and vapor. Time employed.	30	20	18	16	15	20	35 to 50
Quite cloudy, but lower atmosphere, free from vapors. Time employed......................	50	30	25	20	20	30	50 to 70

It is impossible at present, to state precisely the time required to expose the plate in the camera at all seasons of the year; but the above table, drawn up by Mr. D. W. SEAGER, of this city, and which coincides in general with the observations of others, may prove useful as a guide to experimenters. The time will necessarily decrease as the summer months approach. Much, however, depends upon the selection of the view; a white marble edifice, for instance, requires less time than darker buildings. ED.

DAGUERREOTYPE APPARATUS.

Complete sets of the Daguerreotype Apparatus, containing every thing necessary for the process, of different sizes,

Price from 25 to 50 Dollars,

FOR SALE BY DR. J. R. CHILTON,

PRACTICAL CHEMIST, &c. No. 263 BROADWAY,

NEW-YORK.

J. R. C. respectfully announces to the public that he also keeps for sale at his establishment, a general assortment of Philosophical and Chemical Apparatus, Chemical Preparations, and every thing requisite for the study of Chemistry, and other branches of Natural Philosophy : among which, are the following :

Pixii's French Air Pumps, with glass barrels ; Air Pumps, with brass barrels, single and double, of various sizes ; together with the various Apparatus used with them.

Large and small Plate Electrical Machines.
"   "   "   "   with Cylinders, and the various Apparatus connected therewith.

Electro-Magnets, mounted on frames, of all sizes, capable of supporting from 20 to 3000 lbs.

Page's Compound Magnet and Electrotome, for producing brilliant sparks and powerful shocks. The same instrument with a contrivance attached, by which the intensity of the shock can be modified at pleasure, thereby rendering it one of the most convenient instruments for the application of Electricity as a remedial agent in the cure of disease, and for physiological experiments.

Small working models of Electro-Magnetic Machines of various kinds, and a great variety of Electro-Magnetic instruments for the purpose of illustrating the theory of Electro-Magnetism.

Galvanic Batteries, on Professor Faraday's plan for deflagration, &c. Calorimotors, of different sizes.

Gasometers, Compound Blowpipes, Portable Pneumatic Troughs, Mercurial do.; White and Green Glass Retorts and Receivers, Flasks, Tubes, and Evaporating Dishes ; Porcelain Retorts, Tubes, and Evaporating Dishes, Funnels, Mortars, &c.

Iron Retorts of different sizes ; Bell Glasses, plain and stoppered ; Graduated Bell Glasses, Tubes, &c. Bolt Heads, Woulf's Apparatus, Glass Alembecs, Stoppered Funnels, Precipitating Jars.

Nooth's Apparatus for Impregnating Water with Carbonic Acid.

Glass Condensing Syringes, or Fire Pumps, Magic Lanterns, with Astronomical and other Slides.

Porcelain, Wedgewood, Hessian, and Black Lead Crucibles, Muffles and Cuppels.

Berzelius' Spirit Lamps, with Stands and Rings, Glass Spirit Lamps, &c. &c.

An assortment of Platina vessels, such as Crucibles, Capsules, Spoons, Forceps, &c. Platina Wire and Foil.

Models of Crystals in wood, in boxes containing one hundred different forms.

Raspail's Microscopes.

A large collection of Minerals, for sale by the single specimen, or in sets.

INSTRUCTIONS
IN
THE DAGUERREOTYPE.

MR. SEAGER,

Room No. 13 Clarendon House, 304 Broadway, New-York,

GIVES INSTRUCTIONS IN THE DAGUERREOTYPE.

Having produced proofs of the art as early as September last, he presumes upon the numerous experiments he has made, to possess a thorough knowledge of it, and adduces his specimens as evidence of his successful mode; an excellent result, being in fact the only true criterion of a careful manipulation and of a complete knowledge of all the circumstances of the art.

The Terms for a thorough induction by practice, of the mode of taking views of the greatest minuteness, and of rich and pleasing tone of color, twenty dollars; and of taking interiors, and portraits, thirty dollars.

PORTRAITS taken in a few minutes, at a very moderate cost, with the addition of groups of statuary, or other pleasing adjuncts, to form an agreeable picture.

Mr. SEAGER invites his friends and the public to call and see his proofs of this beautiful Art.

PLATES FOR THE DAGUERREOTYPE.

Messrs. CORDUAN, PERKINS & CO. Nos. 28 and 30 Cherry Street, New-York, manufacture and keep constantly for sale, PLATES for the Daguerreotype, of different sizes.

PROSPECTUS

OF THE

AMERICAN REPERTORY

OF

ARTS, SCIENCES AND MANUFACTURES;

EMBRACING

RECORDS OF AMERICAN AND OTHER PATENT INVENTIONS; ACCOUNTS OF MANUFACTURES, ARTS, &c. OBSERVATIONS ON NATURAL HISTORY AND MECHANICAL SCIENCE;

Philosophical and Literary Essays;

AND A SUMMARY OF PUBLIC DOCUMENTS CONNECTED WITH ALL THESE SUBJECTS;

CONTAINING, ALSO,

THE TRANSACTIONS OF

THE MECHANICS' INSTITUTE OF THE CITY OF NEW-YORK;

LYCEUM OF NATURAL HISTORY OF THE CITY OF NEW YORK;

THE GENERAL SOCIETY OF MECHANICS AND TRADESMEN;

NATIONAL ACADEMY OF DESIGN;

THE JERSEY CITY LYCEUM;

AND OTHER SCIENTIFIC INSTITUTIONS.

EDITED BY JAMES J. MAPES,

Professor of Chemistry and Natural Philosophy in the National Academy of Design; Honorary Member of the Scientific Institute of Brussels, of the Royal Society of St. Petersburgh, and of the Geographical Society of Paris; Member of the Lyceum of Natural History of New-York; Honorary Member of the National Academy; Corresponding Secretary of the Mechanics' Institute, &c. &c.

In offering this Periodical to public attention, it is doubtless the first duty of the Editor to point out his reasons for the undertaking. Almost every class of citizens has a journal devoted to its particular interests, through which it can freely communicate information, and advocate its claims to legislative protection, public notice, &c. The Mechanics, only, are without such a vehicle of communication; and it not unfrequently happens, that particular styles of manufactures are confined to particular districts, simply for want of a proper medium of disseminating information. The wants and interests of Mechanics are thereby rendered but *secondary;* whereas they are entitled to, and should receive, a *first* place in public respect and consideration. Another remarkable fact is, that notwithstanding more original inventions are patented in this country than in *all others,* there exists not a journal containing the specifications of patents to which the public may refer for full information.

It is impossible, in a prospectus, which must necessarily be brief, to give any thing beyond a mere synopsis of the plan proposed to be followed in carrying out the present publication.

THE FOLLOWING SUMMARY WILL EXPLAIN THE OBJECTS OF THE EDITOR:

1. A course of Papers on Mechanical and other Drawing, viz: Isometrical Projection, Plane and Orthographic Drawing, and Perspective.

2. Modes of calculating Mechanical Powers, Weight of Metals by Measurement, Tensions of Metals, &c.

3. Practical Illustrations of the comparative strength of materials used for mechanical purposes, arranged in tabular form.

4. Treatises on Mechanical Laws in general.

5. Papers on Chemistry, Natural Philosophy, Astronomy, &c.; and Mathematics as applied to Mechanical purposes.

6. Specifications of Patents.

7. Occasional Literary Essays, Notices of the Fine Arts, &c.

8. Papers on the Progress of Practical and Theoretical Mechanics.

9. Biographical Notices of Distinguished Inventors.

These, with other items of smaller importance, and which occasion may call forth, will constitute the staple of the work now offered to the public.

The progress of the useful Arts and of Mechanical Science should be so exhibited, that they shall strongly attract the attention, not only of those immediately interested therein, but of the public generally. At present this is not the case, for the obvious reason, that most publications on such subjects are rendered so obscure by the too great use of technical terms, that only persons of liberal education, after much scientific reading, are able to comprehend them.

It is intended to illustrate every important invention or discovery, requiring it, with Engravings on Steel, Copper, Stone, or Wood; and occasionally an engraved portrait of some distinguished inventor will be given, serving to illustrate the state of the Fine Arts in this country. The work will be published in Monthly Numbers, each number containing from 80 to 100 pages.

TERMS. Four dollars per annum, payable in advance on delivery of the first number. No subscription will be received for a shorter term than six months. Single numbers thirty seven and a half cents each.